HOW OUR SPACE PROGRAM USES ION PROPULSION

CHILDREN'S PHYSICS OF ENERGY

BABY PROFESSOR

EDUCATION KIDS

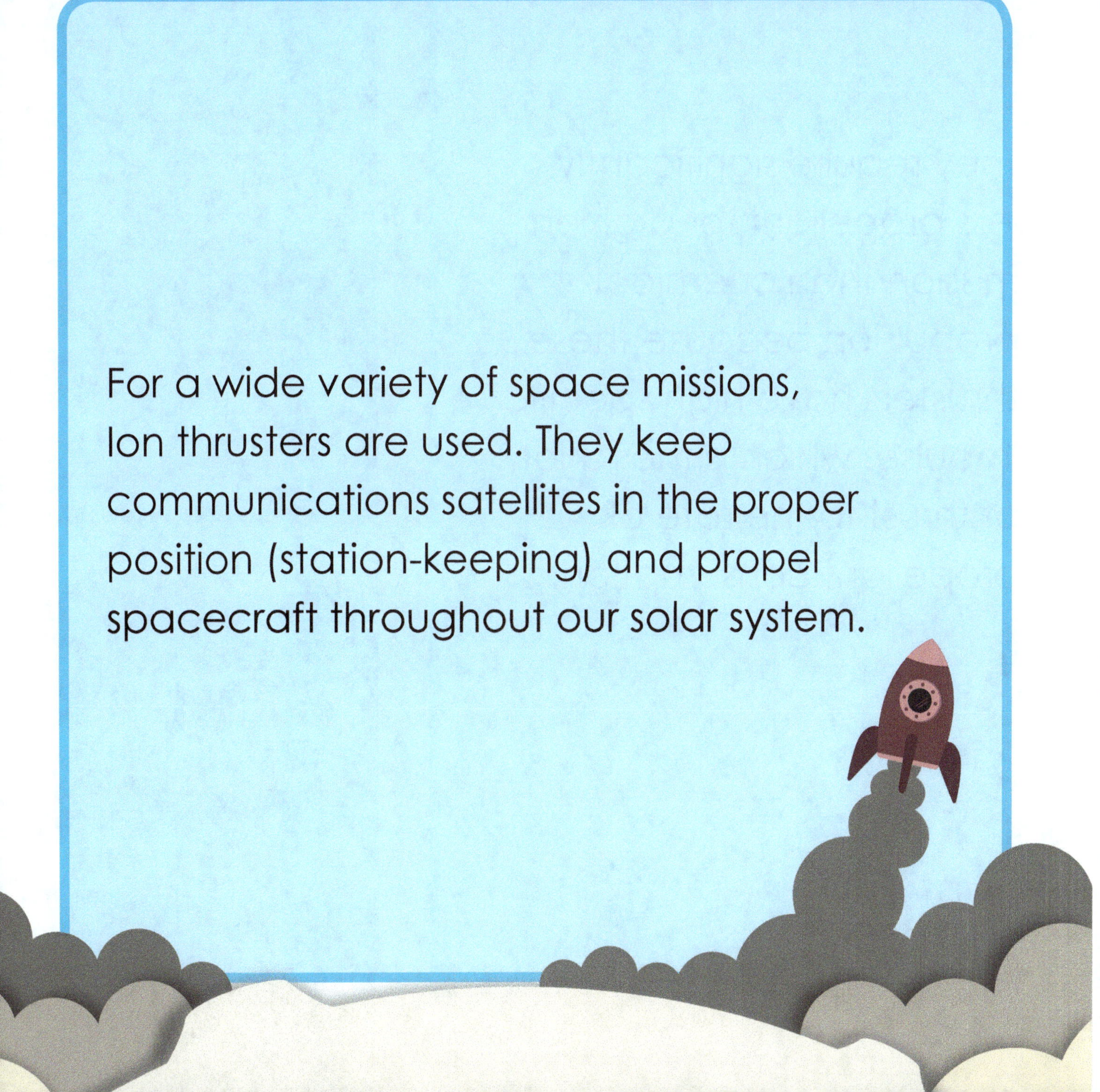

For a wide variety of space missions, Ion thrusters are used. They keep communications satellites in the proper position (station-keeping) and propel spacecraft throughout our solar system.

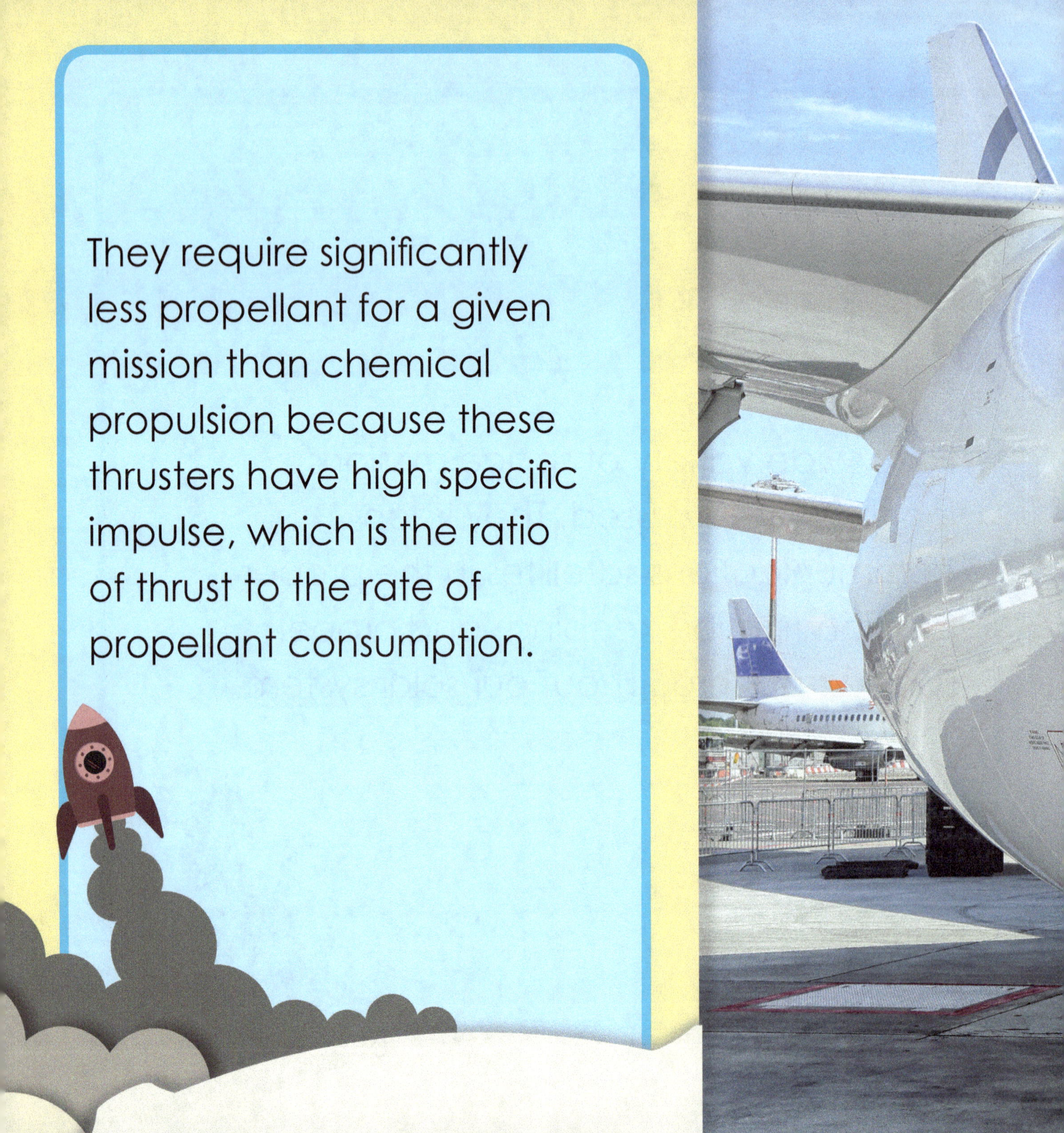

They require significantly less propellant for a given mission than chemical propulsion because these thrusters have high specific impulse, which is the ratio of thrust to the rate of propellant consumption.

In some cases, ion propulsion is used for spacecraft that cannot carry sufficient chemical propellant to accomplish their missions.

HOW ION PROPULSION WORKS?

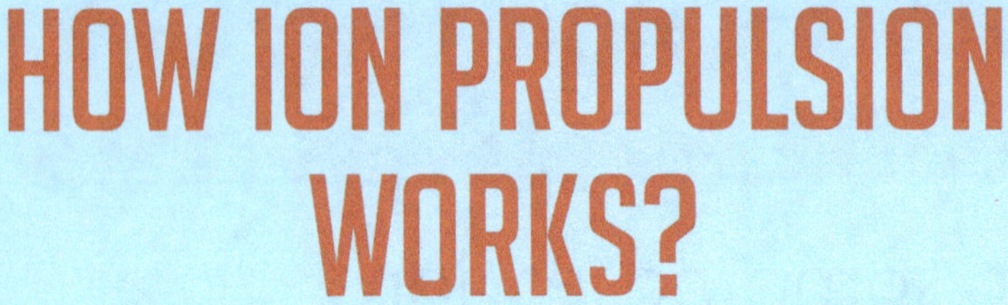

To produce ions, an ion thruster ionizes propellant by adding or removing electrons.

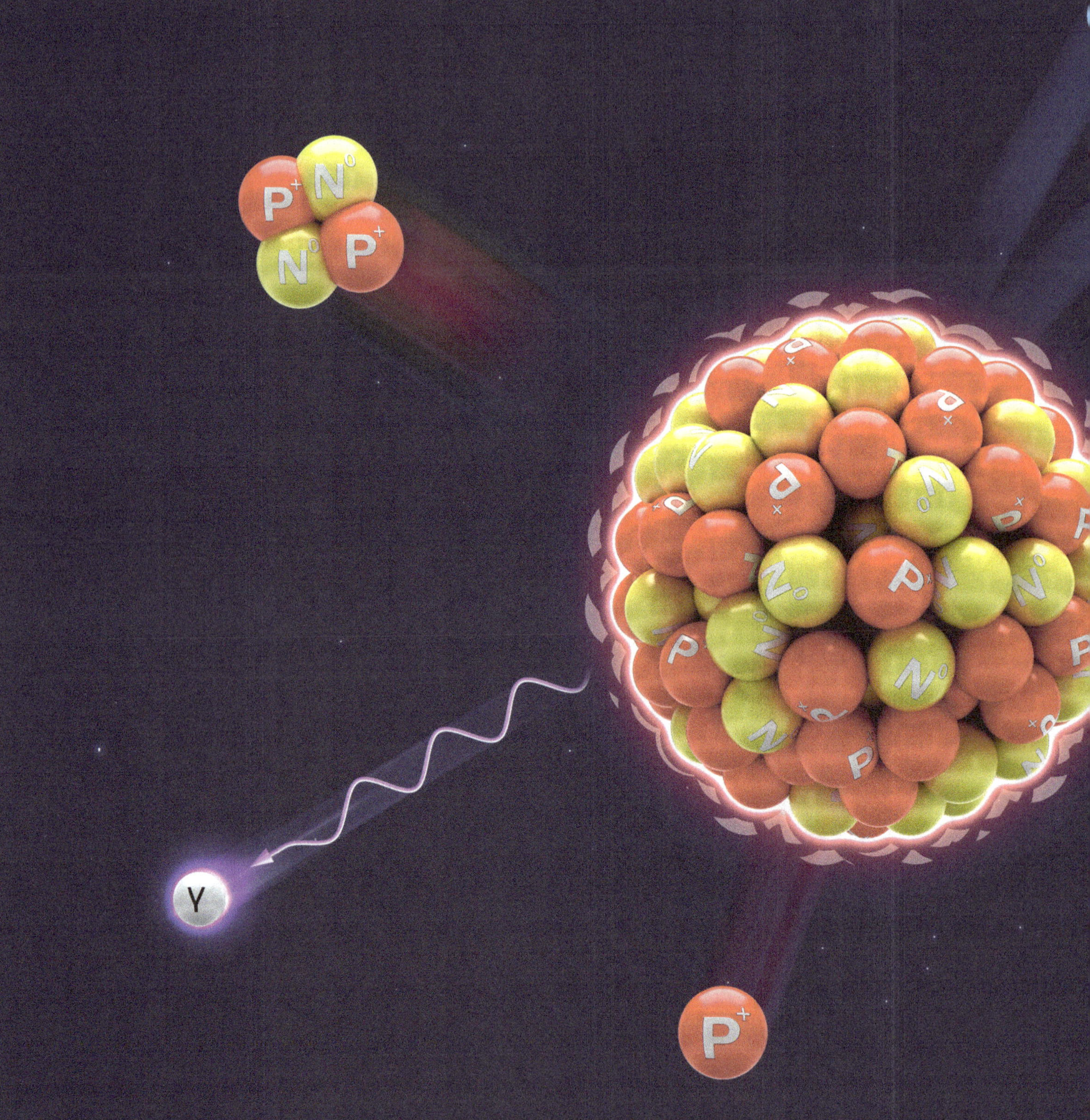

P+
N0
N0
P+
P+
N0
P+
N0
N0
P+
N0
P+
N0
P+
N0
N0
P+
N0
Y
P+

Most thrusters ionize propellant by electron bombardment, which sends high-energy electrons that have a negative charge to collide with a propellant atom that has neutral charge, thus releasing electrons from the propellant atom that result in a positively charged ion.

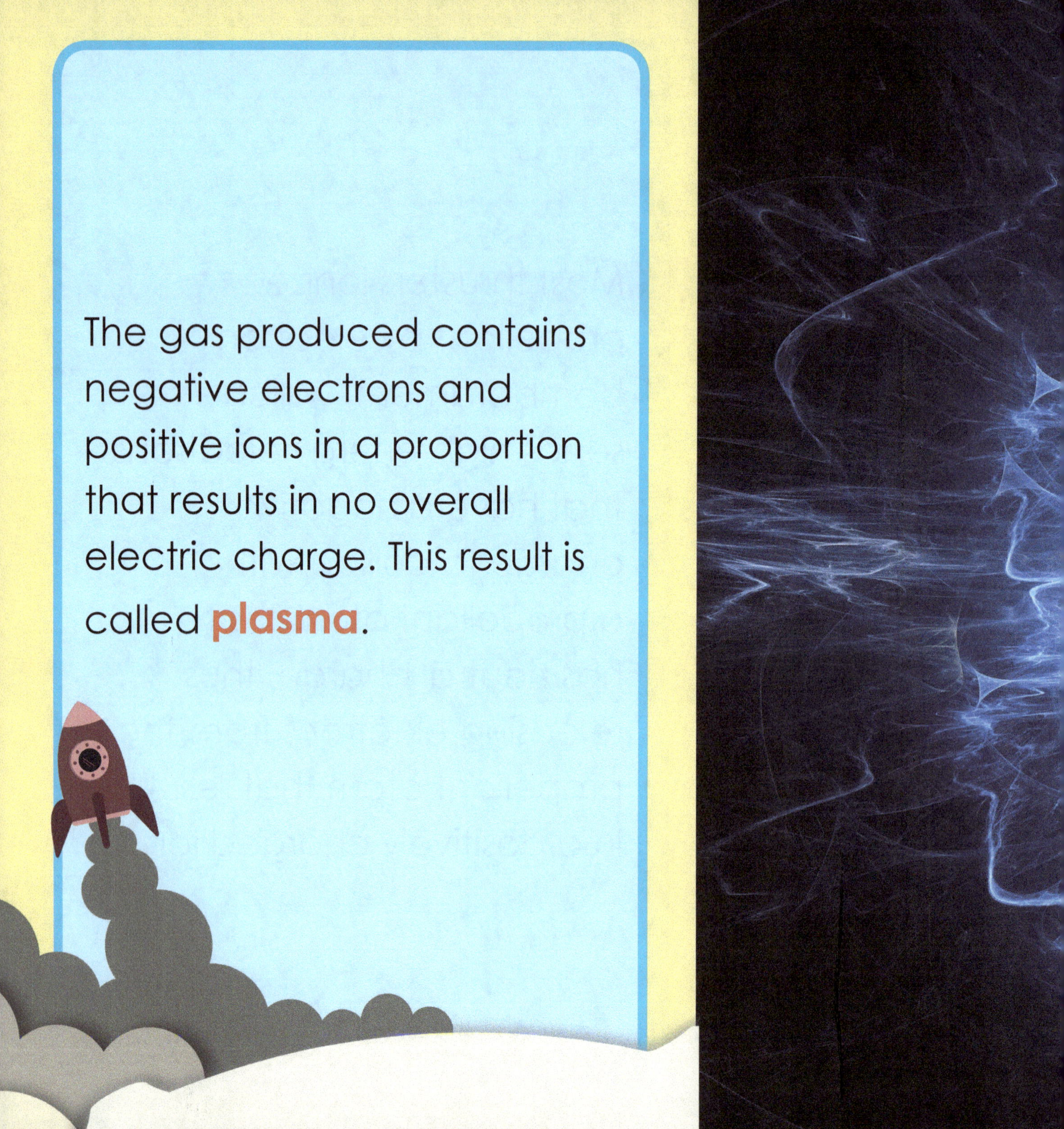

The gas produced contains negative electrons and positive ions in a proportion that results in no overall electric charge. This result is called **plasma**.

Though plasma has some gaseous properties, it is affected by electric and magnetic fields. We can see the effects of plasma in fluorescent light bulbs and lightning.

Xenon is the most common propellant used in ion propulsion. This has a high atomic mass and easily ionizes, thus generating a desirable level of thrust when ions are accelerated.

54
Xe
Xenon
131.293

It has a high storage density and also is inert. Therefore, it is well suited for storing on spacecraft. A thermionic discharge (a flow of electrons over a metal surface, or discharge cathode, which is in contact with a vacuum) delivers electrons in most ion thrusters.

The discharge chamber walls attract the electrons produced by the discharge cathode. The voltage applied by the thruster's discharge power supply charges these electrons to a high positive potential.

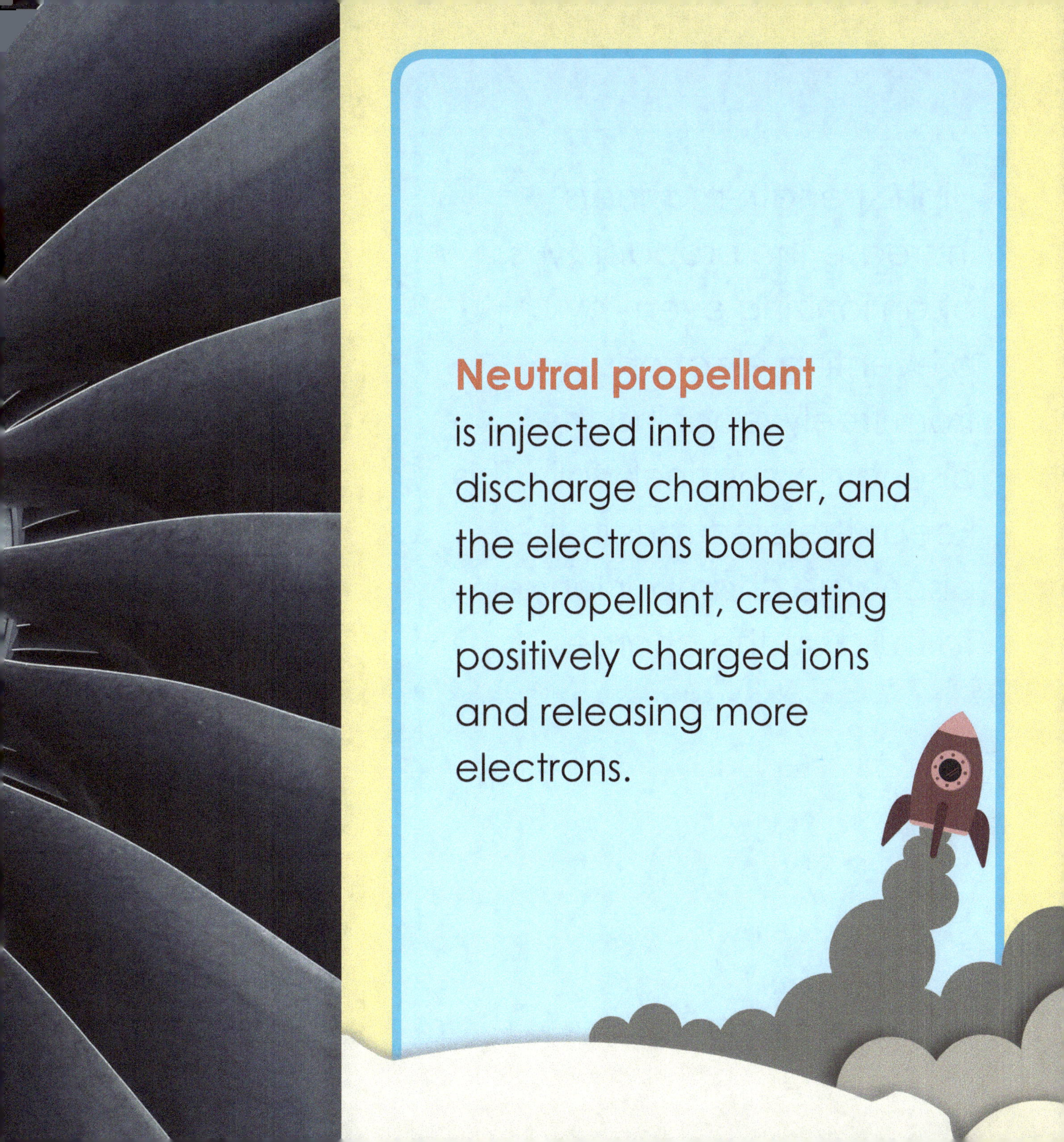

Neutral propellant
is injected into the
discharge chamber, and
the electrons bombard
the propellant, creating
positively charged ions
and releasing more
electrons.

High-strength magnets increase the probability of an ionizing event by preventing electrons from freely reaching the discharge channel walls. This keeps the electrons in the discharge chamber longer, to build up the charge.

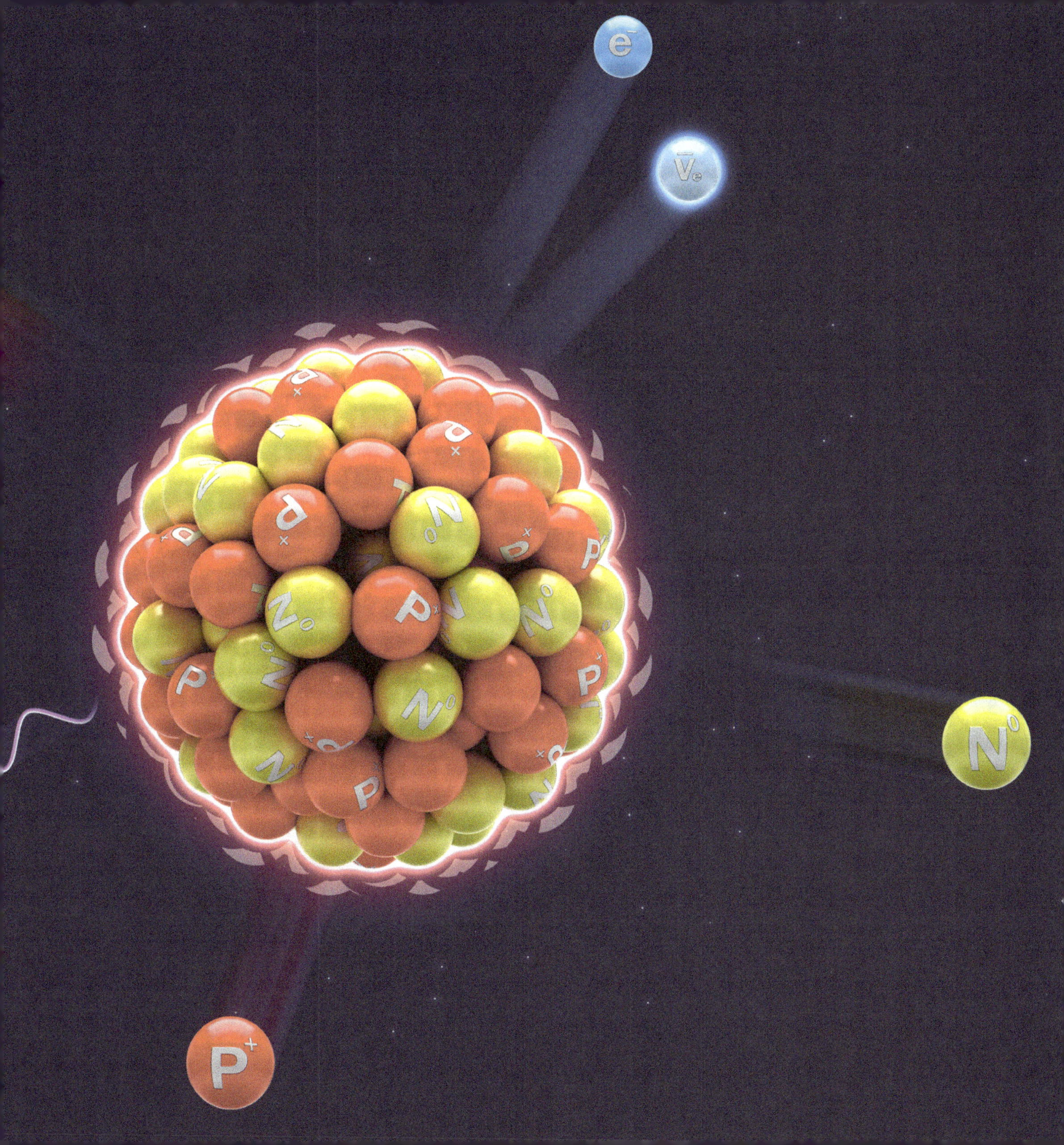

e⁻
Ve
P⁺
N⁰
P⁺
N⁰

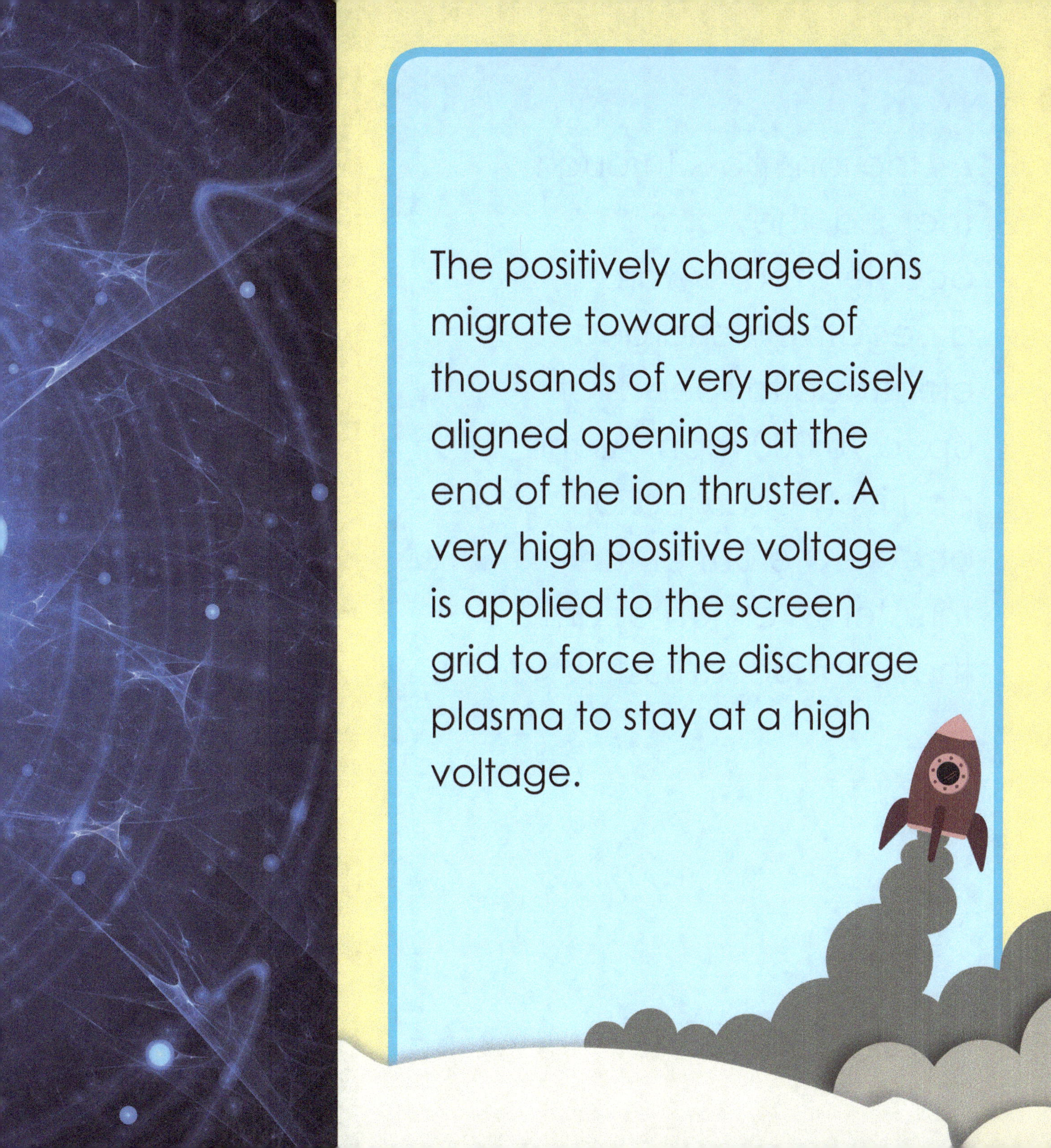

The positively charged ions migrate toward grids of thousands of very precisely aligned openings at the end of the ion thruster. A very high positive voltage is applied to the screen grid to force the discharge plasma to stay at a high voltage.

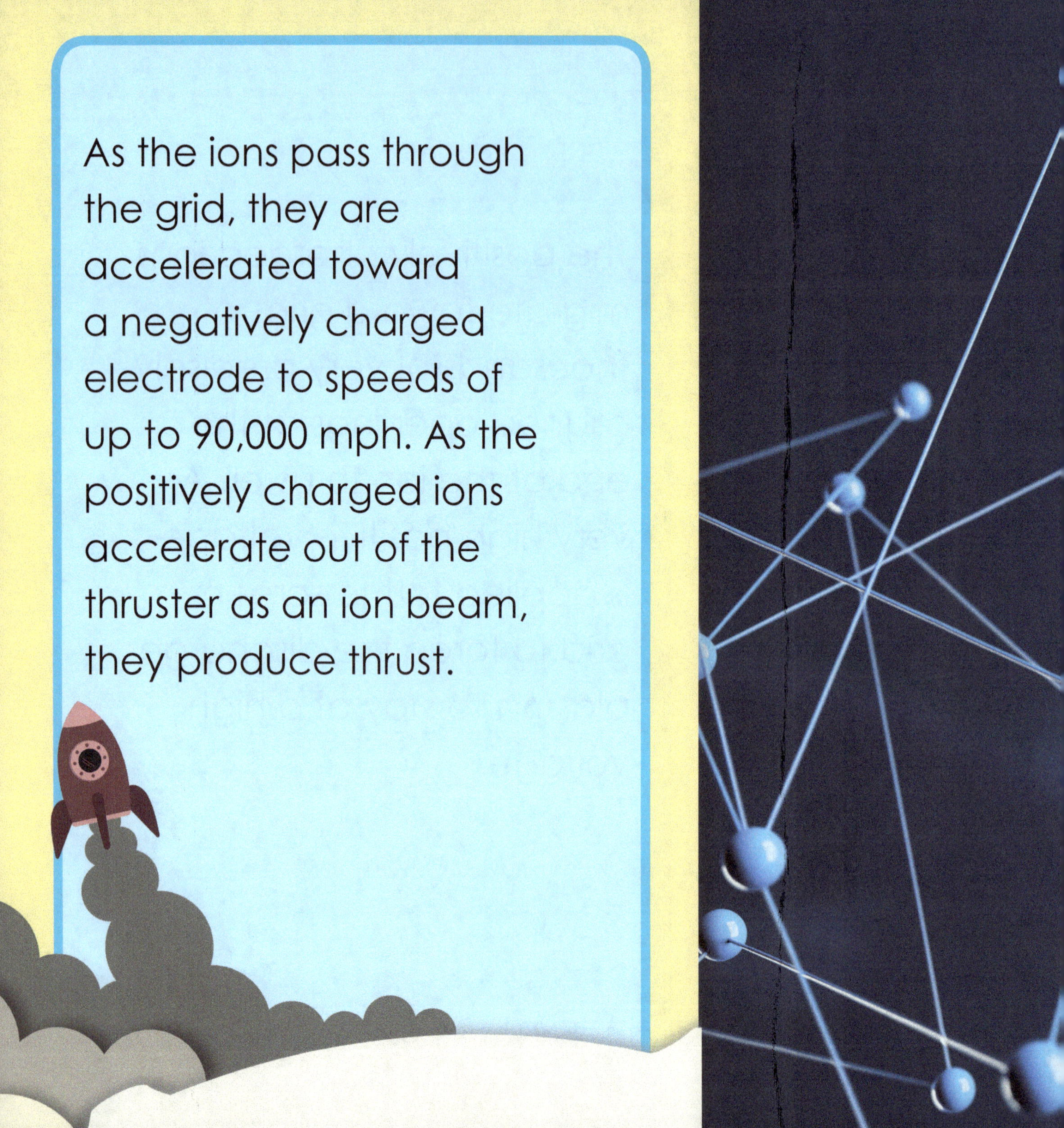

As the ions pass through the grid, they are accelerated toward a negatively charged electrode to speeds of up to 90,000 mph. As the positively charged ions accelerate out of the thruster as an ion beam, they produce thrust.

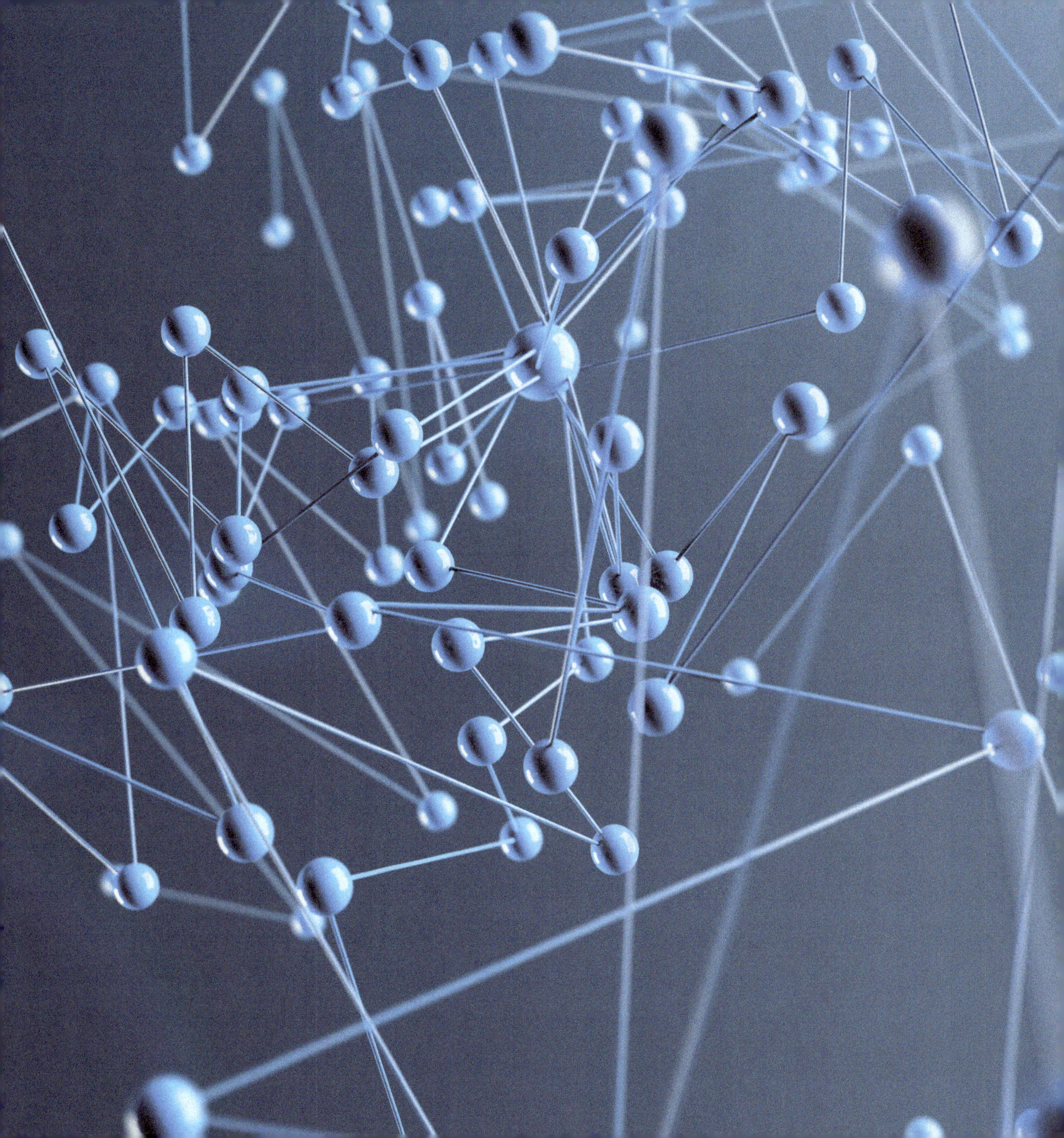

Another hollow cathode, the neutralizer, expels an equal amount of electrons to make the total charge of the exhaust beam neutral. Without this second stream, the spacecraft would build up a negative charge and then eventually ions would be drawn back to the spacecraft, reducing thrust.

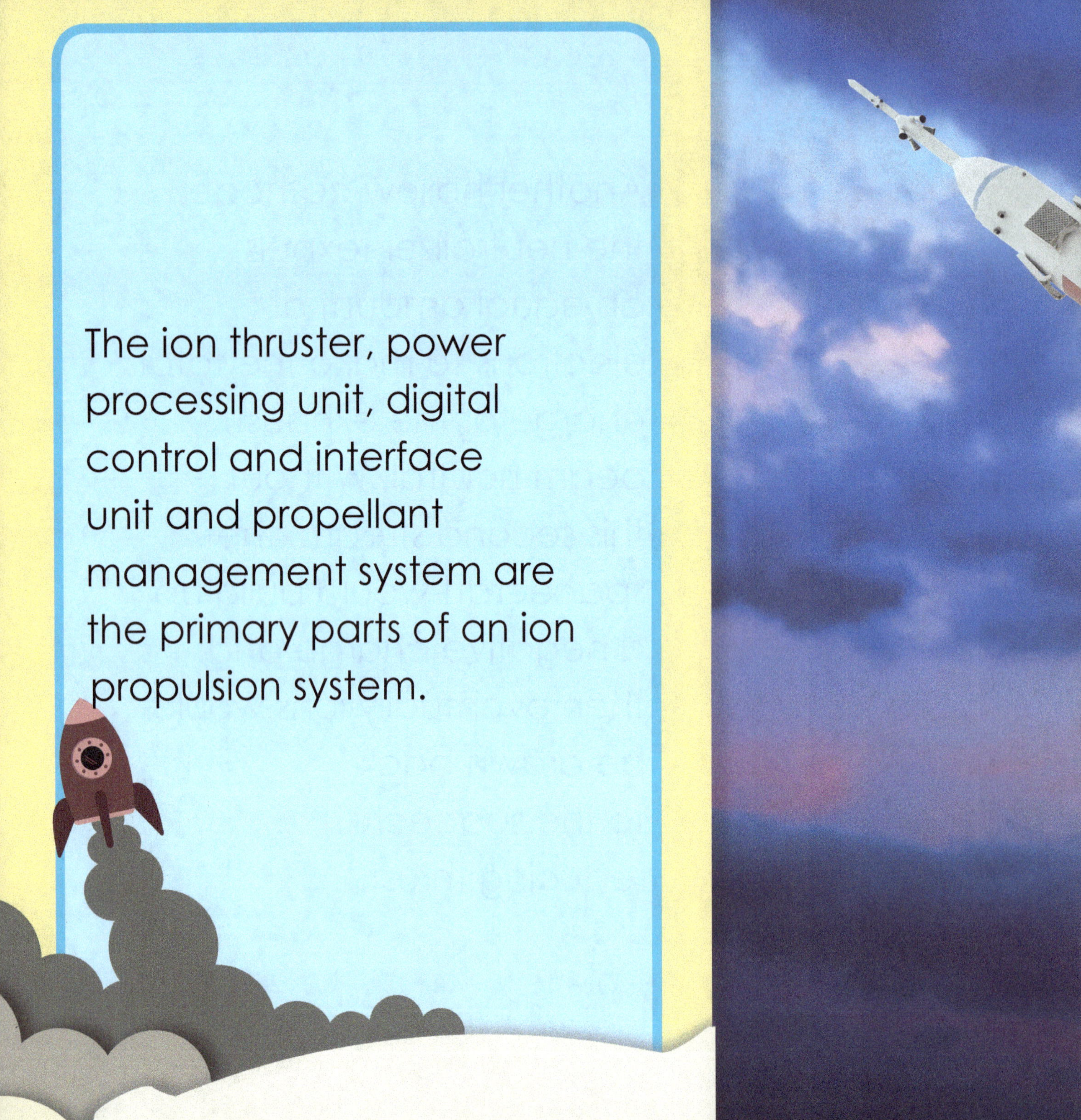

The ion thruster, power processing unit, digital control and interface unit and propellant management system are the primary parts of an ion propulsion system.

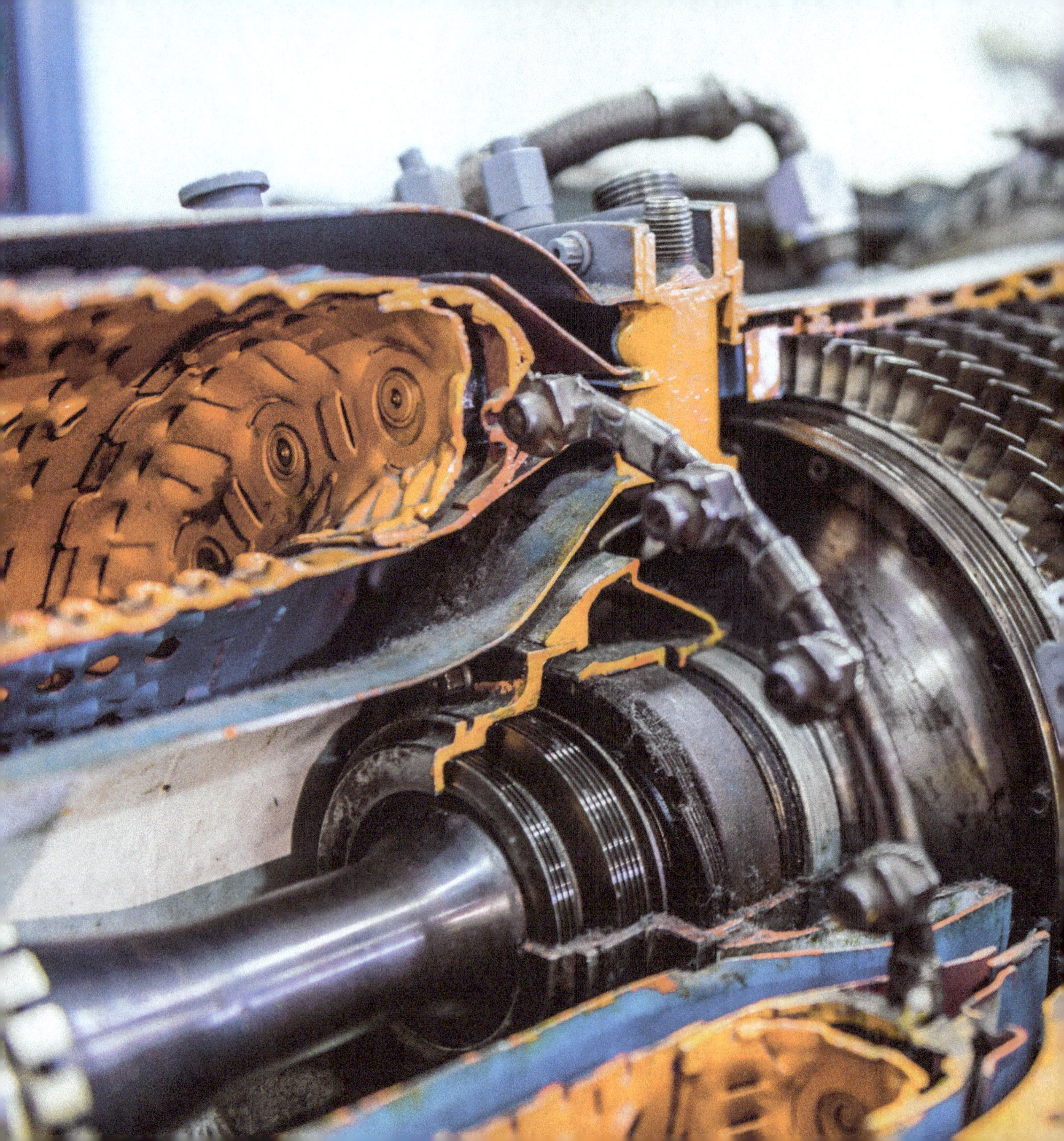

From a power source,
which is usually solar cells
or a nuclear heat source,
the power processing unit
converts the electrical power
into the voltages needed
for the hollow cathodes to
operate, to bias the grids,
and to provide current
needed for the ion beam to
be produced.

The management system may be divided into a high-pressure assembly to reduce the xenon pressure from the higher storage pressures in the tank, and a low-pressure assembly that measures accuracy for the ion thruster components. The control and interface unit communicates with the spacecraft computer and controls and monitors system performance.

Now, we all know that going to outer space is not as easy as riding a bus going to school. Thanks to physics for making a transportation to outer space possible!

Visit

BABY PROFESSOR
EDUCATION KIDS

www.BabyProfessorBooks.com
to download Free Baby Professor eBooks
and view our catalog of new and exciting
Children's Books